A Community Shakespeare Company
Edition of

The Taming of the Shrew

Original verse adaptation by

Richard Carter

"Enriching young lives, cultivating community"

A Community Shakespeare Company
Edition of

The Taming of the Shrew

Original verse adaptation by

Richard Carter

"Enriching young lives, cultivating community"

iUniverse, Inc.
New York Lincoln Shanghai

A Community Shakespeare Company Edition of
The Taming of the Shrew

iUniverse books may be ordered through booksellers or by contacting:

iUniverse
2021 Pine Lake Road, Suite 100
Lincoln, NE 68512
www.iuniverse.com
1-800-Authors (1-800-288-4677)

ISBN-13: 978-0-595-38932-2 (pbk)
ISBN-13: 978-0-595-83314-6 (ebk)
ISBN-10: 0-595-38932-5 (pbk)
ISBN-10: 0-595-83314-4 (ebk)

Printed in the United States of America

CONTENTS

CAST OF CHARACTERS

BAPTISTA MINOLA — a wealthy citizen of Padua, father of Katherine and Bianca

KATHERINE ~ *Alexandra* — the shrew

BIANCA — her younger sister

PETRUCHIO — a wealthy gentleman of Verona, suitor to Katherine

LUCENTIO (pretends to be Cambio) *Bianca's tutor* — a young gentleman of Pisa, suitor to Bianca

HORTENSIO (pretends to be Litio) *Bianca's tutor* — a gentleman of Padua, suitor to Bianca

GREMIO — a wealthy older gentlemen of Padua, suitor to Bianca

GRUMIO — servant to Petruchio

TRANIO, BIONDELLO *Ethan* — servants to Lucentio

CURTIS, NATHANIEL, PETER — servants in Petruchio's country home

VINCENTIO — a wealthy merchant of Pisa, father to Lucentio

MERCHANT — coming from Mantua; impersonates Vincentio

1ST WIDOW, 2ND WIDOW — wealthy ladies of Padua

1ST TAILOR, 2ND TAILOR — visitors to Petruchio's country home

HABERDASHER — a hat maker, visitor to Petruchio's country home

SERVANT — in the house of Baptista Minola

PRIEST, ATTENDANTS, GUESTS — at the wedding

(*This play should run approximately one hour and fifteen minutes, without intermission.*)

Lucentio(me) Switches with Tranio (his servant)—(Ethan).

ACT I, scene 1:

(A STREET IN PADUA. ENTER LUCENTIO AND TRANIO)
me   *ethan*

LUCENTIO
Tranio, my trusty squire, you know it's long been my desire
To visit fruitful Lombardy, the pleasant garden of Italy.
Therefore, have I Pisa left, and to study I am come to Padua.

TRANIO — *Ethan*
Gentle master, ~~I can see how glad you are,~~
~~And glad am I for you.~~ But let us not
~~Be devoted only to Aristotle.~~
~~With logic and mathematics, be not overzealous:~~
~~Remember, you can study pleasure as well as~~
~~Metaphysics.~~ No profit grows where no pleasure is tane.
In brief sir, study, but don't be insane.

LUCENTIO
Gramercies, Tranio, well dost thou advise.
But who comes here? What beauty meets mine eyes?

(ENTER BAPTISTA WITH HIS TWO DAUGHTERS, KATHERINE AND
BIANCA; GREMIO, A PANTALOON, AND HORTENSIO, SUITER TO
BIANCA. LUCENTIO AND TRANIO CONCEAL THEMSELVES)

BAPTISTA
Gentlemen, importune me no farther,
For I shall not bestow my youngest daughter,
Bianca, before I have a husband for Katherine, her sister.
If you sir, or you, should find that you can't resist her,
I give you leave to court her.

GREMIO
To cart her, rather.

KATHERINE
(TO BAPTISTA) Is this your last resort, sir?
To make a wench of me amongst these mates?

1

HORTENSIO
No mates for you. I'll not be knocking at your gates.

KATHERINE
Faith, sir, I'm glad to hear that,
For I'd be forced to remove your hat
And comb your hair with a three-legged stool!
Father, I'll not be married to such a fool!

BAPTISTA
Gentlemen, I mean what I have said:
No man shall have my Bianca till Katherine is wed.

KATHERINE
"My Bianca." Thank you, sir, whose Kate am I?

BIANCA
Mine, sister. Be content: I shall die
A maid so long as you remain unwed. Father, to your pleasure I humbly show
My obedience. To my books and instruments I go.

LUCENTIO
(ASIDE) Tranio! Did you hear the goddess speak?

KATHERINE
You're such a mouse, Bianca. Squeak, squeak, squeak, squeak!

(EXIT BIANCA)

BAPTISTA
Gentlemen: schoolmasters will I employ
For fair Bianca, my gentle joy.
If you know any such men, who in music are clever,
Or cunning in poetry, send them hither.
Katherine, I give you my leave to stay.

(EXIT BAPTISTA)

KATHERINE
And I trust I may go, too! I'm not one to wait all day
For others to tell me what I may and may not do!

(EXIT KATHERINE)

HORTENSIO
What a woman!

GREMIO
What a ~~devil!~~ *bear!*

TRANIO
(ASIDE) What a shrew!

HORTENSIO
Signor Gremio, a word I pray:
We have been rivals for Bianca's love, and may
Be again; but for now, we must work as a team
To achieve one thing. Here is my scheme:
We must get a husband for her sister, Kate.

GREMIO
A husband! A devil! Is there any man you hate
So much that you'd wish that she-wolf on his head?
She'll eat a man alive! He'll wish he were dead!

HORTENSIO
Tush, Gremio, there's plenty of men who'll find her sweet as honey,
So long as her father gives them lots of money!
Are we agreed then? For this shrew we'll find a suitor?

GREMIO
Agreed. But if we fail, can we just shoot her?

(EXEUNT GREMIO AND HORTENSIO)

LUCENTIO
Oh, Tranio! I burn, I pine, I perish!
Modest Bianca I must have, must hold, must cherish.

Counsel me, Tranio, I know you'll assist me:
How can we make it so she can't resist me?

TRANIO
Master, saw you nothing else but her charms?
Heard you nothing at all to raise your alarms?

LUCENTIO
I saw her coral lips move; with her breath she perfumed the air.

TRANIO
Master, I pray you awake! There's something you need to hear:
Her elder sister is so curst and shrewd
That their father must have her out of his brood.
No one may wed Bianca; you're out of luck.
Till he rids himself of the monster, you're stuck.

LUCENTIO
But marked you not? For Bianca he seeks a tutor.
Disguised as her schoolmaster, I could be her suitor!
No one here knows my name, or my face, or my hose…
I've got it, Tranio! Take off your clothes!

TRANIO
But Master…

LUCENTIO
There's no time to waste, give me thine!
I'll wear the servant's clothes, you shall wear mine.

TRANIO
I'll be the master?

LUCENTIO
Yes!

TRANIO
I'll have a servant for me?

LUCENTIO

Yes! When ~~Biondello~~ comes, ~~he waits~~ on thee.

they

the Servants

TRANIO

Done.

(THEY EXCHANGE CLOTHES)

~~Because I love so well Lucentio,~~

~~I am content to be Lucentio.~~

LUCENTIO

Be so, because Lucentio loves a maid.

TRANIO

Just one thing: when I'm master, do I still get paid? —

Laugh, and gently push Ethan

(ENTER BIONDELLO)

LUCENTIO

Here comes Biondello. Rogue, where have you been?

BIONDELLO

This is the strangest thing I've ever seen.

Which is man, which is master? Pray, sir, what's the news?

LUCENTIO

Listen closely, Biodello, there's no time to lose:

Your fellow Tranio, to save my life,

Puts on my apparel and helps me to a wife.

You must obey him as you would me:

I am now Tranio; Lucentio he.

BIONDELLO

But Master...

LUCENTIO

Shh! You must call *him* Master; call me fellow.

TRANIO

Think of me as the first violin, him the cello.

BIONDELLO
You the violin, he the cello…what am I in this trio?

TRANIO
The viola.

LUCENTIO
Music, maestro! Allegro, con brio!

(EXEUNT)

ACT I, scene 2:

(OUTSIDE HORTENSIO'S HOUSE. ENTER PETRUCHIO AND HIS MAN GRUMIO)

PETRUCHIO
Grumio, from Verona I take my leave.
Here in Padua friends will receive
Us. I think this is Hortensio's home.
Knock me soundly here, to tell him I am come.

GRUMIO
Knock you here, sir? What am I, that I should knock *you*?
I'm just your poor servant; give me something else to do.

PETRUCHIO
Villain, I say knock me at this gate,
And rap me well, or I'll knock your knave's pate!

GRUMIO
Knock you here? Rap you well? Sir, if I knock you first,
I know what comes after, and who gets the worst.

PETRUCHIO
Faith, if you'll not knock, then by heaven, I'll ring:
By your ears, I'll wring you, Grumio! Now sing!

GRUMIO
Help! Open up! My master is mad!
He thinks my ears are a doorbell! Egad!

(ENTER HORTENSIO)

HORTENSIO
How now, what's the matter? Why it's Grumio, my old friend!
And Petruchio! Welcome to Verona! What happy gale sends
You from Padua?

PETRUCHIO

Such wind as scatters young men from their home:
To seek wives and fortune, 'round the world we roam.
My father, Antonio, is deceased; I his sole heir,
With crowns in my purse have lately come here,
To wive and thrive as best I may.

HORTENSIO

Hmm. You've come here seeking a wife, you say?
Petruchio, old friend, I wish you no ill;
There's a maiden here with looks that could kill,
And if her glance isn't fatal, her tongue may be.
Still, she's very beautiful, take it from me.

PETRUCHIO

Is she rich?

HORTENSIO

Very rich.

PETRUCHIO

Then what else should matter?
I would take her to wife were she mad as a hatter!
Be she beast, fish, or foul, be she curst or a shrew,
If she comes with a generous dowry, she'll do.

GRUMIO

Look you, sir, he tells you flatly his mind:
It matters not if she's cold or unkind.

HORTENSIO

She's intolerable curst, and shrewd beyond all measure.

PETRUCHIO

Peace, Hortensio. Such faults are mended by sufficient treasure.
Tell me her father's name, and I'll go courting.
If she chide as loud as thunder, that makes it sporting.

HORTENSIO

Baptista Minola, a gentleman no longer young.
His daughter Katherine is renowned for her scolding tongue.

PETRUCHIO
I will not sleep, Hortensio, till I see her.

GRUMIO
If she comes to know him as I do, I would not want to be her.
She may perhaps call him names, she may even scold him,
But if *he* rail against *her*? Sir, you should behold him.

HORTENSIO
I'll go with thee, Petruchio, for in Baptista's keep is my treasure:
His other daughter, Bianca; a jewel beyond all measure.
No man may woo her till her sister finds a mate;
Bianca is prisoner of the accursèd Kate.

GRUMIO
Katherine the curst!
A title for a maid, of all titles the worst!

HORTENSIO
Petruchio, if you will do me this favor,
Bianca may yet be freed. We can save her!
Offer me to Baptista, disguised as a schoolmaster,
So that in secret I may woo Bianca, and avert this disaster.

(ENTER GREMIO, ~~AND LUCENTIO~~—*DISGUISED AS CAMBIO, A SCHOOLMASTER*)

GRUMIO
Who goes there?

HORTENSIO
'Tis Gremio, the rival of my love.
Stand aside with me, and we'll watch his next move.

(THEY STAND ASIDE)

GREMIO
See that you read no other lectures to her but books of love.

LUCENTIO
Of course. I'll woo her like a turtledove,
I'll plead for you as if you were in my place.

GREMIO
She is sweeter than perfume, more delicate than lace.

GRUMIO
And he is an ass.

PETRUCHIO
Peace Grumio.

HORTENSIO
Mum!
(COMING FORWARD) God save you, Signor Gremio. Gentlemen, come.

GREMIO
Well met, Hortensio. Do you know where I'm going?
To Baptista Minola, about a seed that I'm sowing.
I promised to inquire about a schoolmaster
For fair Bianca, and I know she will cast her
Eye favorably on this young scholar:
He's well read in poetry, and books that will enthrall her.

HORTENSIO
'Tis well, and I have met a gentleman musician,
Who in the practice of music will be her physician.
So shall I not be behind in my duty
To fair Bianca, my beloved, my cutie!

GREMIO
My fair one, *my* belovèd, as my deeds shall prove!

HORTENSIO
Gremio: 'tis not now time to vent our love.
Listen to me, I'll tell you good news for us both:
This gentleman will woo curst Katherine!

GREMIO
By my troth!
Hortensio, have you told him all her faults?

HORTENSIO
He says he can make her do summersaults.

PETRUCHIO
I know she is irksome, brawling, and cold,
Why, that's nothing, masters, if she comes with enough gold.

GREMIO
Oh, sir, such a life with such a wife, I would wish on no man,
But if you've a stomach to it, I'll assist you in all that I can!

PETRUCHIO
Why came I hither but to find me a wife?
A little din from a woman frights me not. By my life,
Have I not in my time heard lions roar,
Heard the sea, puffed with winds, rage at my door?
Have I not heard cannon in the field, thunder in the sky?
Do you think a woman's tongue holds any fear for me?

GREMIO
Hortensio, this gentleman is happily arrived.
But for him, our wooing might not have thrived.

HORTENSIO
There's one catch: I've promised we will pay his expenses.

GREMIO
Of course! Quick, before he comes to his senses!

(ENTER TRANIO—*DISGUISED AS LUCENTIO*—AND BIONDELLO)

TRANIO
Gentlemen, God save you. If I may be bold,
Which way to Baptista Minola's, of whom I've been told.

BIONDELLO
He that has two fair daughters, so we hear.

GREMIO
Both are fair to look upon, but have you heard more?

HORTENSIO
Do you come as a suitor, and if so, for which one?

PETRUCHIO
If you seek her that chides, you had better have done.

TRANIO
I love no chiders, sir. Biondello, let's away.

GREMIO
Not without more words. Gentlemen, make him stay.

TRANIO
Why, what's this? Are not the streets as free for me as for you?

HORTENSIO
That depends, sir, on what you intend to do.
Will you woo the fair Bianca, this man Gremio's love?

GREMIO
The intended of this man Hortensio? Don't move.

TRANIO
Softly, masters! If you be gentlemen, do me this right:
May not a maiden have more suitors without a fight?
If her face should launch a thousand ships,
May not a thousand men yearn for her lips?

LUCENTIO
Sirs, I pray you, give him some lead.
I know by his looks he will prove a jade.
He's a broken down horse, you have nothing to fear.
His suit will enhance your own, that much is clear.

GREMIO
What say you, gentlemen?

PETRUCHIO
Leave him to me.
Sir, the eldest daughter is mine, do you see?
And the youngest, whom you desire, can't be wed
Till her older sister is safe in my bed!

TRANIO
If this be so, all our fates depend on you.
I must, like these gentlemen, wait my turn to woo.

HORTENSIO
You say well, and since you profess to be a suitor,
Well met! Let Bianca decide which of us is cuter.

GREMIO
O excellent motion!
Fellows, let's be gone, to show our devotion!

HORTENSIO
All for one, one for all! And let it be so!
Three cheers for our savior, Petruchio!

Ha-ra, Ha-ra, Ha-ra! (arm punching up in the air)

(EXEUNT)

ACT II, SCENE 1:

(BAPTISTA MINOLA'S HOUSE. ENTER KATHERINE, AND BIANCA WITH HER HANDS TIED)

BIANCA
Good sister, wrong me not, nor yourself to make a slave of me:
Unbind my hands; I want only to behave for thee.
I'll pull off my finery, I'll do whatever you command me.
I know my duty to my elder; I know you cannot stand me.

KATHERINE
Of all thy suitors, tell me which one you love best?
Which one will be your husband? Which do you detest?

BIANCA
Believe me, sister, of all the many men I've met,
I never have beheld that special face, I swear, not yet.

KATHERINE
You lie! Is it not Hortensio?

BIANCA
No.

KATHERINE
Then Gremio. Tell me true!

BIANCA
Sister, if you fancy them, I'll give them both to you!
I prithee, Kate, untie my hands, that I may woo them for thee.
You do but jest…

(KATE STRIKES HER)

KATHERINE
No, I detest,
Indeed, I do deplore thee.

(ENTER BAPTISTA)

BAPTISTA
How now! What insolence! Poor girl, she weeps. There, there.
(UNTIES HER HANDS)
Go in, Bianca, ply thy needle. Meddle not with her.
For shame, Katherine, devilish spirit! What harm did she do you?

KATHERINE
Her sweetness mocks me, that's enough. I'll be revenged. (TO BIANCA) Boo!

(BIANCA SCREAMS, FLEES.)

BAPTISTA
You dare to do this in my sight? You put me to the test!

KATHERINE
I see she is your treasure, sir. I know you love her best.
She must have a husband; *I* must dance barefoot at her wedding!
Talk not to me! I'll sit and weep!

(EXIT KATHERINE)

BAPTISTA
Oi! You must be kidding.
Was ever man thus grieved as I? But how now, who comes here?

(ENTER GREMIO, PETRUCHIO, LUCENTIO—*DISGUISED AS CAMBIO;*
HORTENSIO—*DISGUISED AS LITIO;* TRANIO—*DISGUISED AS LUCEN-
TIO;* AND BIONDELLO, BEARING A LUTE AND BOOKS)

GREMIO
Good morrow, neighbor Baptista. We bring you news of good cheer.

PETRUCHIO
God save you, sir, have you not a daughter Katherine, fair and gentle?

BAPTISTA
I have a daughter Katherine, sir. (ASIDE) Gremio, is he mental?

GREMIO
(TO PETRUCHIO) You are too blunt, sir. Try again.

PETRUCHIO
Trust me: I know what I'm doing.
(TO BAPTISTA) I'm Petruchio, sir, a gentleman of Verona, come here to go a-wooing.
Hearing of your daughter Kate, her wondrous mild behavior,
I've come to see her for myself, for I cannot help but crave her.
And for entrance to your house, I offer this man, Litio, as tutor.
Accept him, or you do me wrong, for I would be her suitor.

BAPTISTA
Y'are welcome both, but as for Kate, I think you do not know her.
You will see her mildness for yourself.

PETRUCHIO
'Tis well, I pray you show her.

GREMIO
Baptista, I too have a gift: Cambio, a scholar.
I present him to teach fair Bianca, if only you would call her.

BAPTISTA
I thank you Gremio, welcome Cambio. (TO TRANIO) And you, sir, I would know you.

TRANIO
Lucentio, of Pisa, sir, I too have something to show you:
(BIONDELLO STEPS FORWARD WITH A LUTE AND BOOKS)
Toward the education of your daughters, I present these tokens of esteem,
For I have heard of Bianca: to win her is my dream.

(ENTER A SERVANT)

BAPTISTA
Take these tutors to my daughters, bid them use them well.

SERVANT
Yes, sir. Gentlemen, come this way: behold the ~~gates of Hell.~~ Wolf's den.

(EXEUNT SERVANT, HORTENSIO, LUCENTIO)

PETRUCHIO
Signor Baptista, I pray forgive me if I woo in haste,
I'm heir to my father's fortune, and I have no time to waste.
All my lands and goods would be your daughter's, if I should lose my life.
What dowry do you offer, if I take her to wife?

BAPTISTA
After my death, half my lands; twenty thousand crowns for now.

PETRUCHIO
'Tis a match! Draw up the papers. I'll love your Kate, and how!

BAPTISTA
But will she love you, Petruchio? As yet you have to woo her.

PETRUCHIO
I woo not like a babe. Fear not: my loving will undo her.

(ENTER HORTENSIO WITH HIS HEAD BROKE)

BAPTISTA
How now, friend, why look you pale?

HORTENSIO
This is the work of your daughter!

PETRUCHIO
By the world, it is a lusty wench! I'm glad now that I sought her!

BAPTISTA
Signor Petruchio, will you go with us, or shall I send Kate to you?

PETRUCHIO
I'll woo her with some spirit when she comes. Send her here, I pray you, do.
(EXEUNT ALL BUT PETRUCHIO)
Say she rail at me with bitter words, I'll tell her she sings sweetly.
Say she frown, or growl, or bid me pack, I'll thank her for asking discreetly.
(ENTER KATE)

But here she comes, what shall I call her? My wife? My love? My dear?
Petruchio, speak: Good morrow, Kate, for that's your name I hear.

KATHERINE
Well have you heard, though somewhat deaf; they call me Katherine that do
name me.

PETRUCHIO
You lie: you are called plain Kate. I am Petruchio, born to tame thee!
You're bonny Kate, and dainty Kate, and sometimes Kate the curst.
Kate of my consolation, of all Kates, Kate the worst.
Hearing thy mildness praised in every town, thy virtue and beauty sounded,
Myself am moved to woo thee for wife, because you're so well rounded.

KATHERINE
Let them that moved you hither, remove you hence if they prize you,
I knew you were a movable the moment I laid eyes on you.

PETRUCHIO
Why, what's a movable?

KATHERINE
A three-leggèd stool.

PETRUCHIO
Thou hast hit it! Come Kate, sit on me!

KATHERINE
Asses are made to sit on. For myself, I'd rather spit on thee.

PETRUCHIO
Come, come, you wasp, you're too angry.

KATHERINE
If I be waspish, best beware my sting.

PETRUCHIO
My remedy then is to pluck it out (HE PINCHES HER BEHIND. SHE
SCREAMS)
Why Kate, how sweetly you sing.

(SHE STRIKES HIM) I'll cuff you if you strike again.

KATHERINE
So may you lose your arms. (HE TAKES HOLD OF HER)
If you strike me, you are no gentleman. Is this how you display your charms?

PETRUCHIO
Nay, come Kate, you must not look so sour.

KATHERINE
It is my fashion when I see a crab.

PETRUCHIO
Why, where's a crab?

KATHERINE
Look in the mirror.

PETRUCHIO
Mean you my face? I'm not so drab.
Nay, hear you, Kate, you escape not me. I find you passing gentle.
'Twas told me you were rough and sullen. Why, you're just sentimental.
You're pleasant, gamesome, courteous; you're sweet as springtime flowers.
With mildness you entertain your wooers; I could hold you like this for hours.

(SHE BREAKS AWAY)

KATHERINE
Go fool, handle your servants so. They must take your command, not me.
Keep you warm.

PETRUCHIO
I mean to, in thy bed. Kate, I will marry thee.
In plain terms, your father has consented, your dowry is agreed.
You may fight and spit, you may make denial, but really, there's no need.
I see your beauty; I'm a husband for you. By this light, I like you well.
I am he that was born to tame you. If you can love me, time will tell.

(ENTER BAPTISTA, GREMIO AND TRANIO)

BAPTISTA
Signor Petruchio, how speed you with my daughter?

PETRUCHIO
It's impossible I should fail.

BAPTISTA
How now, daughter? In your dumps? You look like you're in jail.

KATHERINE
You dare to call me daughter, sir? You show yourself a tender father,
By wishing me to marry this lunatic! I would marry a wild pig rather!

PETRUCHIO
Father, 'tis thus: yourself and the world have misjudged this modest beauty:
She's temperate as the morn, and we will be wed. This Sunday would well suit me.

KATHERINE
I'll see thee hanged first!

GREMIO
Petruchio: she says she'd rather see you dead.

TRANIO
Is this how you tame her?

PETRUCHIO
Be patient, gentleman. I promise, we will be wed.
I choose her, and she chooses me. Her shrewishness is an act.
Alone, how she hung about my neck, and held me. That's a fact!
O you are novices! You know not women. They say one thing and mean another.
In company she pretends to be curst, but alone, you should see us together!
Gentlemen, father, wife, adieu. Sunday is practically here.
I must go to Venice to buy new clothes. Kiss me, Kate! (SHE REFUSES) See you soon, my dear.

(EXEUNT PETRUCHIO AND KATHERINE SEPARATELY)

BAPTISTA
God send you joy, Petruchio, 'tis a match! We'll see you on Sunday.

GREMIO
I'd give a lot to see what poor Petruchio looks like on Monday!
Was ever a match made so suddenly?

BAPTISTA
Never mind, at least I'll have quiet.
With Katherine is gone…

TRANIO
If she marries, you mean.

GREMIO
Wait till Sunday: she may start a riot.
But as to your younger daughter, Baptista, I'm your neighbor, and I loved her first.

TRANIO
But I love Bianca more.

GREMIO
You're too young.

TRANIO
You're too old! For her husband, you'd be the worst.

BAPTISTA
Content you, gentlemen, I will settle this strife: which of you can provide for her best?
The man that offers the greatest dowry shall have her; I put you to the test.

GREMIO
As you know, my house is richly furnished, fine tapestries hang on the walls.
At my farm, several hundred milking cows and fat oxen stand in my stalls.
That I'm older than he, I must confess, but if I die, all I own shall be hers.
And while I live, she will be mine only love: Bianca, that fair daughter of yours.

TRANIO
Ho-hum, is that all? For an older man, one would think you'd have more to offer.
I am my father's only heir: four houses in Pisa I can proffer,
Besides two thousand ducats a year, from fruitful lands that we hold.
Have I pinched you Gremio?

GREMIO
(ASIDE) Two thousand ducats! I haven't that much, truth be told.
Baptista, she shall have besides, an argosy now lying in Marseilles.
What, have I choked you with an argosy, lad?
Now what do you have to say?

TRANIO
Why, 'tis known my father has argosies three, and twelve tight galleys more-over.
These I add to my offer, Baptista. What say you now, Gremio, old lover?

GREMIO
Nay, I have offered all that I have.

TRANIO
Then the maid is mine, by your word!

BAPTISTA
I confess, your offer sounds best, Lucentio, if your father's as rich as I've heard.
Let him make me assurance, and on Sunday next, you and Bianca shall be wed.

TRANIO
Assurance? There's no need, I'm still a young man.

GREMIO
Even young men can wind up dead.

BAPTISTA
With your father's blessing, Bianca is yours. Without, she's Gremio's bride.

(EXIT BAPTISTA)

GREMIO

Adieu, good neighbor. I'll let you know if I hear Lucentio has died!

(EXIT GREMIO)

TRANIO

A vengeance on your withered hide! 'Tis in my head to do my master good:
As supposèd Lucentio I must find a supposèd father, somewhere in this neighborhood!
A man to play Vincentio. Oh Lord, what a task! What a bother!
Father's commonly get their children, but this child must go get a father!

(EXIT)

ACT III, scene 1:

(BAPTISTA MINOLA'S HOUSE. ENTER LUCENTIO—*AS CAMBIO;* [*tutor*] HORTENSIO—*AS LITIO;* AND BIANCA)

LUCENTIO [*tutor*]
Foolish fiddler, forbear! How my ears ring! Stop your piteous yowling!
No wonder Katherine crowned you; who could bear your hideous howling!

HORTENSIO
Pitiful philosopher, step aside, your lectures are too boring.
If Bianca spent an hour with you, she'll spend fifty-nine minutes snoring!

LUCENTIO
Preposterous ass, [*fool*] that never in your life have read a book!
She could better study music if it were taught by a babbling brook!

BIANCA
Gentlemen, you do me wrong; in this I have a choice.
I'll learn my lessons as I please; you'll listen to *my* voice.
(TO HORTENSIO) Take you your instrument over there, to see that it's in tune.
His lecture will I study now, your lesson I'll have soon.

HORTENSIO
You'll stop his dribbling drivel as soon as I'm in tune?

LUCENTIO
Ha! That will be never! She'll be with me till June.

(HORTENSIO MOVES OFF)

BIANCA
Where left we off, good Cambio?

LUCENTIO
This Latin, in translation.
Sit closer.

BIANCA
Like this?

LUCENTIO
Closer. Ready?

BIANCA
I'm filled with anticipation.

HORTENSIO
Madam, it's in tune!

(HE STRUMS)

BIANCA
Try again, the treble jars.

LUCENTIO
Spit in the hole!

BIANCA
And stand further off.

HORTENSIO
Far enough?

LUCENTIO
Could you tune it on Mars?
(HORTENSIO MOVES OFF)
Hic ibat, Simois, hic est, Sigeia tellus:
I'm Lucentio, son of Vincentio of Pisa.
Hic steterat, Priami, regia, celsa senis:
I'm disguised like this to fool the old geezer.

BIANCA
Hic ibat, Simois, hic est, Sigeia tellus:
I know you not, trust you not, do not presume, Sir.
Hic steterat, Priami, regia, celsa senis
Dispair not, be patient, I'll give you room, Sir.

HORTENSIO
'Tis in tune now!

(HE STRUMS)

LUCENTIO
All but the bass.

HORTENSIO
The bass is perfect! Cambio, you have a tin ear.
Go peddle your philosophy on Jupiter, it's my turn to sit over here.
(THEY TRADE PLACES)
Madam, you must learn the fingering first, let me show you: hold it so.

LUCENTIO
(ASIDE) Unless I'm deceived, our fine musician has amorous strings to his bow!

HORTENSIO
Let me teach you the notes: do, re, mi…

BIANCA
Sir, I know them.

HORTENSIO
Yet read: there's a lesson within.
I'm Hortensio, not Lito.
Fa, sol: here to woo you.
La, ti: choose me, not him!

BIANCA
Do, re, mi: sir, I know you,
Fa, sol: I'm old fashioned,
La, ti: I like not your inventions.

(ENTER SERVANT)

SERVANT
Mistress, your father calls.

(EXIT SERVANT)

BIANCA
Farewell masters.

HORTENSIO
Wait! You've not yet heard my intentions!

LUCENTIO
Farewell, gentle mistress. Adieu, adieu!

(EXIT LUCENTIO AND BIANCA SEPARATELY)

HORTENSIO
Fie! I like not the way that they parted.
If Bianca casts her eye on that lowlife, she's no match for me. I'm broken-hearted!

(EXIT)

ACT III, scene 2:

(OUTSIDE BAPTISTA'S HOUSE. ENTER BAPTISTA, GREMIO, TRANIO—
DISGUISED AS LUCENTIO; KATHERINE, BIANCA, LUCENTIO—*DIS-
GUISED AS CAMBIO;* PRIEST, GUESTS AND ATTENDANTS)

BAPTISTA
(TO TRANIO) Signor Lucentio, 'tis the appointed day for Katherine to be wed,
Yet we hear not of Petruchio; imagine what will be said!
The guests are here, the priest, the bride: they'll fill up all the room!
What a mockery it will be to have a wedding without a groom!

KATHERINE
The shame is mine. He's a madman! I told you he would falter.
He'll woo a thousand maids like me, then leave us at the altar.
Now the world must point at Katherine, and say, "There's mad Petruchio's wife."

TRANIO
Patience, good Katherine, and Baptista. Petruchio means well, by my life.
Though he be merry, yet he's honest. Though he be blunt, I know he's wise.

KATHERINE
I wish I'd never seen him!

(EXIT KATHERINE, WEEPING, FOLLOWED BY BIANCA AND OTHERS)

BAPTISTA
He's brought tears unto her eyes.

(ENTER BIONDELLO)

BIONDELLO
Master, news! Petruchio comes, dressed in the strangest way!
Like a scarecrow, with mismatched clothing. It's really quite a display.

TRANIO
'Tis some odd humor pricks him on, yet often he wears common things.

BAPTISTA
No matter how he comes, so long as he comes. I've already purchased the rings!

(ENTER PETRUCHIO AND GRUMIO)

PETRUCHIO
Come, where is Kate? I must give her a kiss! Where is my lovely bride?

BAPTISTA
Petruchio? Is that really you? Katherine has just stepped inside.

TRANIO
You are not so well appareled as I might wish you were.

GRUMIO
Fortunately, he's not marrying you.

GREMIO
With any luck, he's marrying her!

PETRUCHIO
Where is Kate? I stay too long from her, 'tis time we were at church.

BAPTISTA
She went in. The guests are all waiting. We feared you had left her in the lurch.

TRANIO
See not your bride, Petruchio, in this unseemly get-up.
Borrow some clothes of mine; I'll see that you're nicely set up.

PETRUCHIO
Nonsense! She'll be married to me, not to what I wear!
I'm a fool to chat with you. Grumio, let's go find her in there!

(EXIT PETRUCHIO AND GRUMIO)

TRANIO
He hath some meaning in his mad attire, I'll try to make him change it.

BAPTISTA
No matter, so long as they wed today.

GREMIO
Yes! Let's not rearrange it!

(EXEUNT BAPTISTA, GREMIO, ~~BIONDELLO~~ Servants, AND OTHERS)

LUCENTIO
Tranio, all goes well! Once Kate is wed, I may have her sister.

TRANIO
~~You forget, you must prove your wealth. On that Baptista will insist, sir.~~
~~I must find a man to impersonate Vincentio, and pretend to be your father.~~
~~Then you may claim Bianca.~~

LUCENTIO
~~What a nuisance! No more of this bother!~~
I must contend with that old man Gremio, and with that amorous musician!
It really is too much to bear for a man in my position!

TRANIO
Have patience, sir, they're no match for us. We'll outwit them with our show.
(ASIDE) Oi! What I go through for my master, the lovesick Lucentio!
(ENTER GREMIO)
~~Signor Gremio, are they married? Did they kiss and say "I do?"~~ —Not you, Tranio

GREMIO
You never saw anything like it: Petruchio's more curst than Kate the shrew!

TRANIO
'Tis not possible!

GREMIO
Nay 'tis true: she's a lamb compared to him!   _gasp
He shouted, he swore, he struck the priest! I tell you, it was grim.
When all was said and done, he kissed her with such a smack,
That the very church did echo! But look, they're coming back.

(ENTER PETRUCHIO, KATHERINE, BIANCA, HORTENSIO—*AS LITIO*; GRUMIO, BAPTISTA, AND OTHERS)

PETRUCHIO
Gentlemen, friends, I thank you all, but we must be on our way.

BAPTISTA
You mean will leave on your wedding night?

PETRUCHIO
I mean we'll leave now, today.
I have business that calls me hither.

KATHERINE
Now, if you love me, stay.

PETRUCHIO
Grumio, my horse!

KATHERINE
Nay, do what thou canst, I will not go today!
Nor tomorrow! Not till I please! Father, he shall stay my leisure.

PETRUCHIO
Go forward all, carouse and feast, but for Kate, my bride, my treasure:
She must go with me, she's my house my barn, my field, my ox, my ass.
Touch her who dare! I'll defend her well. Fear not, my bonny lass!
Grumio, draw thy sword! We're beset with thieves! Rescue her if you be a man!
They shall not touch thee, Kate! Away! I'll save you if anyone can!

(EXEUNT PETRUCHIO, KATHERINE, GRUMIO)

LUCENTIO
Mistress, what think you now of Kate?

BIANCA
That being mad herself, she's madly mated.

GREMIO
'Tis true, I almost died of laughing. Petruchio is Kated!

BAPTISTA
Neighbors and friends, let's go to the feast, though we're lacking a bride and groom.
(TO TRANIO) Lucentio, you take Petruchio's place. Let Bianca take her sister's room.

TRANIO
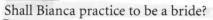
Shall Bianca practice to be a bride?

BAPTISTA
She shall. Let's everyone go.
Drink a health to the madly mated Kate, and her husband Petruchio!

(EXEUNT)

ACT IV, scene 1:

(PETRUCHIO'S COUNTRY HOUSE. ENTER GRUMIO)

GRUMIO
Fie on all mad masters! Was ever man so weary?
I'm sent ahead to warm the house; I'm so tired my eyes are bleary!
I'm so cold my lips might freeze to my teeth, or my tongue to the roof of my mouth!
Considering the weather, if I were a bird, I would have already flown south!
Holla, Curtis!

(ENTER CURTIS)

CURTIS
Who calls?

GRUMIO
A piece of ice. You may slide from my head to my toes.
Good Curtis, a fire.

CURTIS
Is my master coming, and his wife?

GRUMIO
God only knows.

CURTIS
Is she so hot a shrew as she is reported? Tell me Grumio, how goes the world?

GRUMIO
She is hot, the world is cold. A fire, Curtis! Let my toes be uncurled.
Is the supper ready? Are the cobwebs swept? Is everything in order for thy master?

CURTIS
All is ready, good Grumio. I pray you, the news.

GRUMIO
The marriage is a disaster!
Our master and mistress have fallen from their horse, into the dirt; you should see them!
He left her in the mud, she waded out.

CURTIS
I'd rather see than be them.
By this reckoning, he is more shrew than she.

GRUMIO
Aye, that you shall see when he comes.
But where are the others? Call Nathaniel and Peter.

CURTIS
Masters, ho! Come out here, you bums!

(ENTER NATHANIEL AND PETER)

NATHANIEL
Welcome home, Grumio.

PETER
How now, Grumio.

GRUMIO
Welcome, fellows, is all ready? All things neat?

NATHANIEL
All things is ready. How near is our master?

GRUMIO
Too near: like a lion before raw meat.

PETRUCHIO
(OFF) Where be these knaves? Where's a man to take my horse? Why is no one at the door?
Where's Nathaniel? Where's Peter? Where's Grumio, that knave I sent before!

(ENTER PETRUCHIO AND KATHERINE)

GRUMIO
Here, sir.

PETRUCHIO
Did I not bid you meet me outside?
Why, you peasant! You malthorse! You drudge!

GRUMIO
It was their fault, sir, they weren't ready. I pray you, don't hold a grudge.

PETRUCHIO
Fetch my supper! You there, off with my boots! Ow! That hurt! Take that!
(STRIKES NATHANIEL)
Sit down, Kate, be merry. Food, food, food! You there, take my hat!
Where are my slippers? And some water! (PETER SPILLS IT) Why, you villain,
you've got her all wet!

KATHERINE
Patience, sir, 'twas an accident.

PETRUCHIO
Now you see? You've got her upset!
(STRIKES PETER)
Come Kate, sit down. I know you're hungry. What's this meat? 'Tis burnt! And
so's the rest!
(THROWS THE FOOD AND DISHES)
You heedless joltheads, unmannered slaves! You put my patience to the test!

KATHERINE
I pray you, husband, be not so disquiet. The meat looked well, and smelled
delicious.

PETRUCHIO
I tell thee, Kate, 'twas burnt and dried. I'm forbid to touch such dishes.
They upset my stomach, and make me grumpy. I don't want you to see me
angry.
'Tis better we both should fast for this night. We'll feast on love if you're hun-
gry.

(EXEUNT PETRUCHIO, KATE, AND CURTIS)

NATHANIEL
Peter, did you ever see the like?

PETER
Nay, he kills her in her own humor.

GRUMIO
Curtis, is it safe to come out? (ENTER CURTIS) Where are they?

CURTIS
Gone into their chamber.
There he makes her a sermon on self control: he rants and rails, how he swears!
She knows not which way to stand, poor soul. She just sits there silent and stares.
Away, away, he is coming hither.

(EXEUNT. ENTER PETRUCHIO)

PETRUCHIO
Thus have I begun my reign.
And 'tis my hope to end successfully, for 'tis said, "no pain, no gain."
My falcon now is sharp and empty; till she swoop she must not be full fed.
She ate no meat, nor will tomorrow. Just water and cold, stale bread.
Last night she slept not, nor tonight she shall not; I'll find some fault with her pillow.
I'll steal the coverlet, fling off the sheets. By dawn, she's my weeping willow.
All this is done in care of her: to kill her with kindness, as is her due.
Now let him speak, he that knows better, how to tame a shrew!

(EXIT)

ACT IV, scene 2:

(OUTSIDE BAPTISTA'S HOUSE. ENTER TRANIO—*DISGUISED AS LUCENTIO;* AND HORTENSIO—*DISGUISED AS LITIO*)

TRANIO
Is it possible, friend Litio,
That Bianca loves any other but Lucentio?

HORTENSIO
Stand by and watch, I'll show you here,
That Bianca does not hold you dear.

(THEY STAND ASIDE. ENTER BIANCA, AND LUCENTIO—*DISGUISED AS CAMBIO*)

LUCENTIO
Now mistress, do you profit in what I have given you to read?

BIANCA
From this book, "The Art to Love?" Cambio, I do indeed.
May you prove, sir, to be a master of this art.

LUCENTIO
I will, fair Bianca, while you prove mistress of my heart.

(THEY COURT, ASIDE)

HORTENSIO
Ha! You thought that Bianca loved none but Lucentio.

TRANIO
That's true.

HORTENSIO
You see now that she loves another: Cambio, that's who!

TRANIO
Oh, spiteful love! Unconstant woman!
My heart must break, I'm only human.

HORTENSIO
No more am I Litio, the musician that I seemed!
I thought I loved Bianca, but I must have only dreamed!
Know, sir, that I am called Hortensio; this was my disguise.

TRANIO
Signor Hortensio, I have often heard of you, as both a gentleman and wise.
And since we two have seen that Bianca tenders not your affection,
Forswear her love forever, sir, turn your eyes in another direction.

HORTENSIO
I will! I know a wealthy widow, who has long desired my gaze,
I promise you, Lucentio, I'll be married within three days!
Farewell, Signor Lucentio, no more for love I'll tarry,
I'll seek a wife with lots of money. Now *that's* a reason to marry!

(EXIT HORTENSIO. TRANIO JOINS LUCENTIO AND BIANCA.)

TRANIO
Mistress, bless you! You are forsworn! We've sent Hortensio packing.
He'll have a wealthy widow now. It seems he finds you lacking.

BIANCA
God give him joy!

LUCENTIO
Well rid of Litio!

TRANIO
Look, here comes Biondello!

(ENTER BIONDELLO)

BIONDELLO
Tranio! Master! Master! I've found the perfect fellow!
You bid me find a man to play your father, Vincentio.

There's a merchant coming down the hill, you must not let him go!
He's just the right man.

LUCENTIO
But how shall we ever convince him to play this part?

TRANIO
Leave that to me. He'll be glad to do it. Stand aside: here comes the old fart.

(EXEUNT LUCENTIO AND BIONDELLO. ENTER A MERCHANT)

MERCHANT
God save you, sir.

TRANIO
And you. Travel far?

MERCHANT
To Tripoli, by way of Rome.

TRANIO
And from what city, pray you, sir?

MERCHANT
Mantua is my home.

TRANIO
Mantua! God forbid! Come to Padua! Oh, sir, are you careless of your life?
Know you not that Mantua and Padua are locked in civil strife?
'Tis death for anyone from Mantua here! So proclaims the Duke!

MERCHANT
Oh! I feel dizzy, I feel sick! Pray, sit me down before I puke.

TRANIO
'Tis a marvel you have not heard this decree. Sir, it's lucky for you,
That I'm the first one in Padua you found.

MERCHANT
That's true, sir. Thank you, that's true.

Alas, it makes no difference, I have business in Padua still.
I must collect money from someone here. I must deliver this bill!

TRANIO
Well, sir, to do you a courtesy, I'll collect that money for you;
To save your life in this extremity. Yet, I need something too.

MERCHANT
Pray name it, sir, for if you do me this favor, I'm in your debt.

TRANIO
I'm awaiting my father, he should have been here by now. Alas, he's not here yet.
Have you heard of a merchant in Pisa, sir, Vincentio by name?

MERCHANT
I have, if he be a wealthy merchant.

TRANIO
The same, sir; the very same.
He's coming here to pass assurance for me of a worthy dower.
I've been looking for him, he should have been her by now; in fact, this very hour.
I'm to marry Baptista Minola's daughter—the nice one—not the shrew.
I need someone to stand for my father.

MERCHANT
Me?

TRANIO
You'll do, sir. Oh, yes, you'll do.

(EXEUNT)

ACT IV, scene 3:

(PETRUCHIO'S HOUSE. ENTER KATHERINE, GRUMIO, AND CURTIS)

KATHERINE
Did he marry me to famish me? Beggars at my father's door
Receive more food than I do. I don't know how to act anymore!
I never learned to ask for things, they were always given.
Now I'm starved for meat, giddy for want of sleep. Oh, heaven!
I prithee, Grumio, Curtis: go and get me some repast,
Before he kills me with kindness! I know cannot last.

GRUMIO
What say you to a neat's foot?

KATHERINE
I say 'tis passing good.
Right now I'll eat most anything, so it be wholesome food.

CURTIS
I fear what Grumio offers is too choleric a meat.
How say you to some fish?

KATHERINE
By my troth, sir, that sounds sweet!

GRUMIO
Nay, say not so to fish. 'Tis choleric as custard!
What say you to a piece of beef, sliced thick and served with mustard?

KATHERINE
It is a dish that I do love! Pray stop, you make me drool!

CURTIS
Grumio, the mustard is too hot! Tut, tut, don't be a fool.

KATHERINE
Then bring the beef alone, and let the mustard rest.

GRUMIO
You must have beef with mustard: it gives the meat some zest.
So if you will have none, mistress, then I'll bring no beef.

KATHERINE
Then both! Or either! God! Will no one give me some relief?

GRUMIO
Why then, I'll bring the mustard.

CURTIS
No, Grumio, it will not serve.

KATHERINE
Enough! Go! Get you gone, thou false deluding slave!

(SHE BEATS CURTIS, HE EXITS. ENTER PETRUCHIO)

PETRUCHIO
How fares my Kate? How now my sweet? What, art thou depressed?
Nay, be of good cheer! Pluck up thy spirits; I've come to get thee dressed.
We will return to thy father's house, and there we shall be gay.
Come, tailors! Come haberdasher! Let's see this fine array!

(ENTER TAILORS AND HABERDASHER)

HABERDASHER
Here is the cap your worship, just as you had it ordered.

PETRUCHIO
You call this a cap? It's a cockle, a walnut! Look, it's even unbordered!
Away with it! It's a baby's cap, I tell you. Make it bigger!

KATHERINE
This doth fit fine.

HABERDASHER
(ASIDE) It's just what he asked for.

1ST TAILOR
(ASIDE) Don't look at me.

2ND TAILOR
(ASIDE) Go figure.

KATHERINE
I tell you, many a gentlewoman wears such a cap these days.

PETRUCHIO
And I tell you 'twill be out of fashion next week! It's just a craze.

KATHERINE
I trust I may speak for myself, sir, and believe me yet, I will:
(TO HABERDASHER) I'll take one just like this, sir. Can you add a little frill?

PETRUCHIO
Kate, I love you far too well to let you wear that bauble.
He can make you another that's better.

KATHERINE
But...

PETRUCHIO
There, there, Kate. It's no trouble.
But as to your gown: tailors! Bring forth your work, let us see.
You call that a dress?

1ST TAILOR
It's just as you ordered, in every detail.

2ND TAILOR
I agree.
It's according to fashion, the latest style.

KATHERINE
It's gorgeous! It's perfect! It's a jewel.

PETRUCHIO
It looks like it's made for my dog! You rogues! Do you take me for a fool?

KATHERINE
I never saw better. I like it well. It's perfect for me.

TAILORS
That's true.

PETRUCHIO
She's protecting your feelings, thou flea! Thou nit! She's too kind to pay you your due:
It's wretched! It's monstrous! You've marred it, thou unworthy thread! Thou thimble!
Thou rag! Thou remnant! Take it away! Out of my sight, and be nimble!

1ST TAILOR
But it's just what you wanted.

2ND TAILOR
Grumio, speak! You told us how it should be done.

GRUMIO
Nay, I gave you the materials, but orders gave I none.

PETRUCHIO
It matters little, I like it not. The gown is not for me.

GRUMIO
Heavens no, sir. 'Tis for my mistress! On that, we all agree.

PETRUCHIO
Villains, take away these rags! They're not fit to adorn my bride!
Grumio! (ASIDE) See that you pay those fellows, once they're safely outside.
(EXEUNT TAILORS, HABERDASHER)
Well, Kate, that's a pity. We must go to your father's dressed but poorly.
Yet 'tis said that honor appears in plain wrapping. You agree with me, surely.
Let's see, 'tis now just seven o'clock. Grumio, let our horses be saddled!

(EXIT GRUMIO)

KATHERINE
Sir, 'tis not seven. 'Tis two o'clock. I think your brain must be addled.

<u>PETRUCHIO</u>
Say it's seven, Kate, and we'll go there for dinner. It must be what time I say.

<u>KATHERINE</u>
I assure you, sir, it's almost two.

<u>PETRUCHIO</u>
Then we go there not today.

(EXEUNT.)

ACT IV, scene 4:

(OUTSIDE BAPTISTA'S HOUSE. ENTER TRANIO—*DISGUISED AS LUCENTIO;* AND THE MERCHANT—*DRESSED LIKE VINCENTIO*)

TRANIO
Sir, this is Baptista's house, you know what you're to do?

MERCHANT
Aye, I'm to play the father. Here's your boy, does he know too?

(ENTER BIONDELLO)

TRANIO
Fear him not. Holla, Biondello! This is "Vincentio." Art thou done?

BIONDELLO
I've told Baptista your father is come. Lord, this should be fun!

(ENTER BAPTISTA, AND LUCENTIO—*DISGUISED AS CAMBIO*)

TRANIO
Signor Baptista, you are happily met. Here's my father as you requested.

MERCHANT
Sir, I hear good report of you, and 'tis well my son you have tested.
I understand he loves your daughter, and she loves him. I'll not tarry:
I'll secure the match with sufficient dower, if you are content they should marry.

BAPTISTA
Sir, your plain speaking pleases me well. 'Tis a match, if Bianca say so.

TRANIO
I pray you, Baptista, send for her, that her answer we may know.

BAPTISTA
Cambio, fetch Bianca hither.

LUCENTIO

With pleasure, sir! I'll go find her.

BAPTISTA

(TO TRANIO) If Bianca will have you for husband, son, then with wedding vows you may bind her.

(EXEUNT BAPTISTA, MERCHANT, TRANIO)

BIONDELLO

Servant (5)

"Cambio:" if you want my advice, find Bianca, then go to the priest!
Elope with her now! Our deception may yet be discovered by old Baptista.

LUCENTIO

You say well, for the merchant may falter. Or Gremio may yet cause some trouble.

BIONDELLO

Trust me: find the girl, find the church, find the priest! Do it now, sir, on the double!

(EXEUNT)

ACT IV, scene 5

(ON THE ROAD TO PADUA. ENTER PETRUCHIO, KATHERINE, GRU-MIO, AND SERVANTS)

PETRUCHIO
Come on! Once more, toward our father's house. Good Lord, how bright shines the moon!

KATHERINE
The moon? 'Tis the sun! 'Tis not moonlight.

PETRUCHIO
Sweetheart: do you want to get there soon?
I say 'tis the moon.

KATHERINE
'Tis the sun! I'm not blind.

PETRUCHIO
It shall be what I say, don't you see?
If I call it the moon, or star, or whatever; sweet Kate, you must follow me.
For if not, we go not to thy father's house. (TO SERVANTS) Go you fellows, and fetch our things home.

GRUMIO
Mistress, I pray you, say as he says; or back and forth, back and forth we shall roam!

KATHERINE
Forward then, since we've come this far. Be it moon, or sun, what you please.
Henceforth I vow it shall be so for me.

CURTIS
Yes!

GRUMIO
Mistress, you're the bee's knees!

PETRUCHIO
I say it's the moon.

KATHERINE
I know it's the moon.

PETRUCHIO
'Tis the sun.

KATHERINE
God be blessed! 'Tis the sun!

CURTIS
Grumio, I think she shall eat well tonight.

GRUMIO
Then joy to us all! The field is won!

(EXEUNT SERVANTS. ENTER VINCENTIO)

PETRUCHIO
Forward, then! But who comes here? Tell me, Kate, now what do you see?
Hast thou ever beheld a fresher gentlewoman? A lovely maid! What say thee?

KATHERINE
(TO VINCENTIO) Oh young, budding virgin! So fair, fresh and sweet! Happy
parents to so fair a child!

PETRUCHIO
Why, Kate! Art thou mad? This is a man, old and wrinkled! Where do you get
these ideas so wild?

KATHERINE
Pardon, old father, my mistaking eyes, that are so bedazzled by the sun.
Everything I look on seems strange today; I see now you're a man, and a reverend one.

VINCENTIO
Fair sir, merry mistress, I confess your unusual greeting much amazed me at
first.

I'm Vincentio of Pisa, bound for Padua to visit my son, unannounced, unrehearsed.

PETRUCHIO
Pray, what's his name?

VINCENTIO
Lucentio, sir.

PETRUCHIO
Happily met! Why, we're practically related!
Your son will marry my wife's sister! He'll be Bianca'd, as I have been Kated.

VINCENTIO
Here we go again. 'Tis just my luck to meet with two jesters in my travels.

KATHERINE
I assure you, father, 'tis true what he says.

PETRUCHIO
Come along, you may join in our revels!

(EXEUNT)

ACT V, scene 1:

(OUTSIDE LUCENTIO'S LODGINGS. ENTER FIRST GREMIO; THEN BIONDELLO, LUCENTIO—*AS HIMSELF;* AND BIANCA)

BIONDELLO
Softly and swiftly, sir. The priest awaits.

LUCENTIO
Thanks, Biondello, we fly to his gates!

(EXEUNT LUCENTIO AND BIANCA)

BIONDELLO
I'll follow to see that they're safe down the aisle.

(EXIT BIONDELLO)

GREMIO
I marvel that Cambio comes not all this while.

(ENTER PETRUCHIO, KATHERINE, VINCENTIO, GRUMIO, AND SERVANTS)

PETRUCHIO
Sir, here's the lodging where your son stays within.
Farewell.

VINCENTIO
Stay a while. Come, drink a toast with your kin.

(HE KNOCKS)

GREMIO
You were best to knock louder, sir. It's a busy place.

(VINCENTIO KNOCKS LOUDER. MERCHANT LOOKS OUT OF THE WINDOW)

MERCHANT
Hey! What do you want? Get outta my face!

VINCENTIO
Is Signor Lucentio lodged within these walls?

MERCHANT
Who wants to know?

VINCENTIO
Tell him his father calls.

MERCHANT
His father! You liar! Tell me another!
I'm his father.

VINCENTIO
You, his father?

MERCHANT
So says his mother!

PETRUCHIO
(TO VINCENTIO) Why, how now, sir! This is knavery, to steal what a man is named.

MERCHANT
Lay hands on that villain!

(THE SERVANTS TAKE HOLD OF VINCENTIO)

VINCENTIO
How dare you! Let me go! This is madness! Let me go, I've been framed!

(ENTER BIONDELLO)

BIONDELLO
I've seen them to the church; God send them good shipping.
But who's here? My master, Vincentio! Now I'll get a whipping.

VINCENTIO

Come hither, you villain! You rogue! Where have you been?
Have you forgot your old master?

BIONDELLO

Forgot you? Sir, it's the first that I've ever seen
You.

VINCENTIO

Notorious slave! Never seen Vincentio? You're a rascal; how you lie!

BIONDELLO

Vincentio? Why, I see him right now, in that window there up high.

VINCENTIO

I'll show you Vincentio!

(HE BEATS BIONDELLO. THE MERCHANT EXITS FROM THE WINDOW.
ENTER BAPTISTA, AND TRANIO—*DISGUISED AS LUCENTIO*)

BIONDELLO

Help! Murder! The man is mad!

TRANIO

Sir, who are you to beat my servant? (BEATS VINCENTIO)Take that, you cad!

VINCENTIO

How dare you! Who am I? Why you villain, who are you,
If not my son's servant! This place is a zoo!

TRANIO

Pay no attention to this man; he's obviously insane!
I thank heaven my real father doesn't have such a brain.

VINCENTIO

Your real father is a sail-maker!

BAPTISTA

You mistake, sir. He's quite wealthy.

VINCENTIO
Stay out of this, sir, if you want to stay healthy!

MERCHANT
Away, you lunatic! I'm Vincentio! He's my heir,
Lucentio of Pisa. You're as mad as a March hare!

VINCENTIO
I tell you his name is Tranio! For years he's been servant to me!
I brought him up in my house in Pisa, ever since he was three!

TRANIO
Take this man to prison, get him off of the street!
I can't be molested by every raving madman I meet.

BAPTISTA
To prison with him!

GREMIO
Nay, sir, be careful what you do,
Look! Here comes another! He looks like Lucentio too.

(ENTER LUCENTIO AND BIANCA. EXEUNT BIONDELLO, TRANIO, AND
MERCHANT AS FAST AS MAY BE.)

LUCENTIO
(KNEELS) Pardon, sweet father.

VINCENTIO
Nay, is this my real son?

BIANCA
(TO BAPTISTA) Pardon me, father.

BAPTISTA
Bianca! Pray, what have you done?
And where is Lucentio? I see Cambio here.

BIANCA
Cambio, by love, is changed into Lucentio.

LUCENTIO

I am the right son to this man, the right Vincentio.

BAPTISTA

But have you married my daughter without asking my permission?

GREMIO

Children! They're nothing but trouble. I swear, they're the road to perdition.

VINCENTIO

Fear not, Baptista, we will content you. I pray you sir, go in.
(EXIT BAPTISTA)
But Biondello and Tranio: when I catch them, they'll pay for their sin.

LUCENTIO

What they did, sir, myself did enforce them to.
Then pardon them, father.

BIANCA

I pray you sir, do.

(EXEUNT LUCENTIO, BIANCA, VINCENTIO)

GREMIO

So much for my plans, my cake is dough.
I'll find a rich widow, like Hortensio!

(EXIT)

KATHERINE

(COMING FORWARD) Husband, let's follow, to see the end of this ado.

PETRUCHIO

We shall, Kate. But first, I need something from you.
Kiss me, Kate.

KATHERINE

What, here? In the street?

PETRUCHIO

Why not? Are you ashamed of me, Katherine, my sweet?

KATHERINE
Not of you, sir, I swear. But embarrassed to kiss.

PETRUCHIO
Here's my hat then. Come: let's do it like this.
(THEY KISS BEHIND HIS HAT.)
Is not this well? Come, my sweet Kate,
Better once than never, for never too late.

(EXEUNT)

ACT V, scene 2:

(LUCENTIO'S LODGINGS. ENTER BAPTISTA, VINCENTIO, MERCHANT; LUCENTIO AND BIANCA; HORTENSIO AND GREMIO WITH WIDOWS; PETRUCHIO AND KATHERINE; TRANIO, ~~BIONDELLO~~, GRUMIO, AND SERVANTS)

LUCENTIO
At last, fair Bianca, we are all gathered here.
Pray, everyone revel, and be of good cheer!
Time it is when raging war is done;
Welcome to my house, our battles are won!

GREMIO
Speak for yourself, I fear mine has just started.
Hortensio, you told me widows were all warm hearted.

HORTENSIO
For both our sakes, I wish that were true,
At least you're not married yet. What am I to do?

PETRUCHIO
Now, for my life: Hortensio fears his bride!

1ST WIDOW
He needs no help from you, sir.

PETRUCHIO
Roundly replied.

2ND WIDOW
Nor does Gremio, sir, for we've just got engaged.

GREMIO
The more fool, I. She's got me caged!

KATHERINE
Ladies, how mean you? Are your vows of love so weak
That both of you fear to let my husband speak?

1ST WIDOW
We mean that your husband, being troubled by a shrew,
Measures our husbands' woes by his own.

2ND WIDOW
She means you.

KATHERINE
I understand your meanings, and for your husbands I feel sorrow:
They drank the wine of your enticements, but they'll be sober tomorrow.

(EXIT KATHERINE)

BIANCA
Come ladies, let's withdraw. We'll go inside, and leave our "lords and masters."

(EXEUNT BIANCA AND WIDOWS, LAUGHING)

GREMIO
And we'll speak of fires…

HORTENSIO
And floods…

GREMIO
And earthquakes…

HORTENSIO
And marriage!

GREMIO/HORTENSIO
And other disasters!

BAPTISTA
In truth, good son Petruchio, I think you have the veriest shrew of all.

PETRUCHIO
Not so, father, I assure you. Pray, whose lady will come when he call?
For I'll make you a wager, and he shall win whose wife will first do his bidding.

HORTENSIO
Content. What's the wager?

LUCENTIO
Twenty crowns.

PETRUCHIO
Twenty crowns? Lucentio, you've got to be kidding!
I'd venture so much on my hawk, or my hound. Twenty times so upon my Kate!

LUCENTIO
A hundred then!

HORTENSIO
Aye, a hundred crowns says your shrew shall come but late.

PETRUCHIO
Done!

LUCENTIO
~~Biondello,~~ *Servant,* go inside: bid your mistress come at my request.

(EXIT ~~BIONDELLO~~) *Servant*

PETRUCHIO
Now we'll see who knows his wife.

GREMIO
I'm not married yet. Count me out of this test.

(ENTER ~~BIONDELLO~~) *Servant*

LUCENTIO
How now, what news?

Servant (s)
~~BIONDELLO~~
Sir, my mistress sends you word: she cannot come.

PETRUCHIO
How? Is that an answer? She's busy? Strike me dumb.

HORTENSIO
Tranio, go and entreat my wife.

(EXIT TRANIO)

PETRUCHIO
Entreat her? She must come! This man fears for his life.

HORTENSIO
I dare not tell her worse; heaven knows what she would do!
But I warrant I'll fare better than Petruchio and his shrew.

(ENTER TRANIO)

TRANIO
She says she will not come; you have some goodly jest in hand.
She bids you come.

PETRUCHIO
Worse and worse! Her wish is your command!
Grumio, go to your mistress: say I bid her come to me.

(EXIT GRUMIO)

BAPTISTA
I know her answer.

LUCENTIO
So do I.

HORTENSIO
So do I.

GREMIO
We'll see, gentlemen, we'll see.

(ENTER KATHERINE)

BAPTISTA
By my stars, here she comes!

GREMIO
And she's smiling!

KATHERINE
What is your will, sir, that you send for me?

PETRUCHIO
Kate, you look so beguiling.
Go and fetch those wenches three.
If they deny to come, teach them a lesson; beat them hither, and do it straight.

(EXIT KATHERINE)

HORTENSIO
Was that the shrew?

BAPTISTA
Was that my daughter?

PETRUCHIO
That, gentlemen, was my Kate.

(ENTER BIANCA, WIDOWS, AND KATHERINE)

1st WIDOW
What on earth is so important that you send this shrew to hound us?

2ND WIDOW
Indeed, sir why send you hither this tornado to confound us?

BIANCA
Lucentio, what mean you? Will you treat me like a sinner?

LUCENTIO
'Tis no sin to come, Bianca. You've cost me a hundred crowns since dinner.

BIANCA
The more fool you, to wager.

1ST WIDOW
(TO HORTENSIO) And you sir, did you bet too?

VINCENTIO
(TO MERCHANT) Makes a man glad to be single

MERCHANT
I'll say.

PETRUCHIO
Now gentlemen: who's married to a shrew?
Kate, tell these headstrong women what duty they owe their spouses.

KATHERINE
With pleasure. Fie! Unknit those threatening brows, you unkind louses!
A woman so moved is like a fountain troubled, full of muddy, ill-seeming water.
A dog wouldn't dare to drink from you! Who would want you for wife, or daughter?
Thy husband is thy life, the one that cares for thee:
To painful labor he commits his body, on land or on stormy sea.
He craves no other tribute but your fair looks and love;
Shall he live with a foul, contending rebel? Or shall he live with a dove?
Come, come, you feeble worms, who with your eyes cast down,
Would offer war instead of peace, bandy words, and frown for frown:
My head hath been as strong as yours, my heart I think is more;
Our strength can be our weakness, when we seem to be what least we are.
So place your hand beneath your husband's foot, as I dare to on my life,
For I place my trust in him who trusts in me: he as husband, I as wife.

PETRUCHIO
Why, there's a wench! I love thee well! We'll leave them to their fate.
God give you good night! Peace to you all! Come on and kiss me, Kate!

(THEY KISS BEHIND HIS HAT)

CURTAIN

ABOUT THE AUTHOR—
RICHARD CARTER

Richard Carter, MFA, is Co-Founder & Director of the Community Shakespeare Company for young actors. His award-winning plays have been produced from Seattle to London. His verse adaptations of classic literature motivate and enchant actors and audiences, pre-school through adult. Richard lives with his family on an island in Washington State.

After graduating from Vassar College and receiving his MFA in playwriting from the University of Washington, Richard's historical play *Blood and Iron* won Seattle's Jumpstart New Play Competition in 1993, and went on to be presented on the London stage. His musical play, *Winds in the Morning*, received rave reviews at the 1997 Seattle Fringe Festival, and was selected to inaugurate the Port Townsend, WA, Wooden Boat Festival in 2000.

Richard offers his talents in many venues. As Co-founder/Artistic Director of the Community Shakespeare Company, he is one of the few playwrights today with the audacity to work *with* Shakespeare. His adaptations are utterly faithful to the spirit of the original plays, while making them instantly accessible to modern students and audiences.

Community Shakespeare Company itself breaks new ground. Its mission is "to enrich young lives and cultivate community." Richard's leadership motivates parents, mentors, artists, and other volunteers to support and encourage local youth. The result is a dynamic model which can be replicated in schools, organizations, clubs and communities.

Richard and his wife Jeanna live on a small farm where they have been raising their children and practicing sustainable agriculture together since 1988.

NOTES

Lucentio-me

Tranio- Ethan, switches
with Briana in Act III, scene 2

Switch clothing with
Ethan - Act 1, scene 1

Clothing

Lucentio (me) =

When switched with Tranio-
his servant (Ethan) =

NOTES

Clothing = Lucentio &
Tranio & Cambio(tailors,

Lucentio (me) pretends
to be Cambio = switch
hat and vest with
Ethan. = Clothing for
Tranio & Cambio.

Lucentio clothing = Fancy feather
in hat, vest, old-fashioned
shoes, long socks, sweat
pants, nice men's formal
shirt, fancy mustache,
hair up like a man.

NOTES

978-0-595-38932-2
0-595-38932-5